Han~~~~

CAMPER
VAN
MINIMAL

Thank you for a legal purchase of this
handbook! If it wasn't so, please
consider supporting my work here:

WWW.CAMPERVANMINIMAL.COM

minimal

1. of a minimum amount, quantity, or degree.
2. *Art* characterized by the use of simple forms or structures, especially geometric or massive ones.

YOUR PLAN

WITHOUT UNNECESSARY INTRODUCTION

Life is too short to read lengthy introductions. There is too much to see, experience, and understand in this world – be it a journey or a mere willingness to change perspective, broaden the horizon and knowledge. The possibility of living anywhere in the world with minimal consumption of its resources is an argument that speaks for itself.

We'll start by finding out that nothing is fully settled. Each idea, parameter or given centimeter is best considered according to your own needs. All elements are influenced by their size and arrangement, so before getting down to work, I recommend that you read the whole thing first. To perform all the tasks described here, readily available tools powered by batteries are enough, so we only need to find a piece of land, warn potential neighbors about our intentions (it may not cause a smile on their faces, but it may reduce the intensity of those less friendly glances) and start the work.

Any comments or alternative ideas are most welcome and will be taken into account in future editions of this handbook. Let's create the best **CAMPER VAN MINIMAL** together!

I. INSULATION?

IS IT WORTH "ISOLATING"?

WHY: Thermal insulation is the basis of every home... that requires it. The "minimal" version of a mobile home described in this manual is designed to be able to travel comfortably in temperatures between 0°C and 10°C, and live long term on the road when it's between 10°C and about 24°C in full sun (and warmer temperatures, if we can park in the shade). For these purposes, a few centimeters of air already existing in the car between the car body and the panels covering the walls and ceiling from the inside are sufficient. Such a low density of insulation has its advantage: a highly heated car can be cooled down faster in the evening after a hot day. On the other hand, a well-insulated car will require wide-open windows at night or the installation of a large fan for air exchange (e.g. in the roof), which will result in noise and additional electricity consumption. In addition, good insulation makes sense when we heat the air inside, which is associated with additional work, cost, possible emission of exhaust gases, as well as everyday noise of the device. The "minimal" version provides for noiseless, more ecological, direct heating of the human body itself.

However if we decide to increase thermal insulation, we should be prepared for quite time-consuming and tedious work, because each gap (so-called "thermal bridge") will ruin our efforts. As a first layer, I recommend gluing 3-5 cm thick XPS (extruded polystyrene). It doesn't absorb moisture, it's inexpensive and insulates better even than mineral wool. For gluing, it is best to use quick-setting polyurethane glue. Then, using gel contact adhesive, we glue to the first layer of insulation a 5-mm mat made of polyethylene foam covered with a layer of aluminum on both sides. Although it is thin, it reflects heat radiation very well. In order to lay out the floor, we build a wooden frame, which we'll eventually cover, for example, with waterproof wooden pine plywood.

We "hide" the insulation behind the wall panels.

2. WALL DEMOLITION

JUST TO BUILD A BETTER WALL

WHY: The dirtiest tasks are best done before any other work begins. If your car has a wall that separates the passenger compartment from the "trunk", I highly recommend that you consider removing it, or at least the upper half of it. Thanks to this, you can move from the driver's cabin to the residential part without being exposed to any external factors (cold, rain, disturbing others with slamming doors at night, a sudden attack of a hungry bear). All the other pluses will emerge later. Don't worry: in place of a thin metal wall, I'll propose to insert something much better, which will additionally protect us against internal factors, which I'll describe in the next chapter.

HOW TO DO IT: In my van the top of the wall was welded in just a few places, so all you need is a small angle grinder and readiness to be covered with metal filings. Since removing them from myself and from the environment is tiresome, I commissioned this task in a car repair shop. It is worth paying attention to the quality of grinding, as sharp edges will be a danger to you in the future.

TOOLS:
  • angle grinder or visit in a workshop

WARNING: This is a design change of the car – make sure that it's in line with the purpose of your car in your country.

Wall before cutting out.

Wall with a past.

3. BUILDING A WALL

BUT WITH THE SPIRIT OF TIME:
A MOBILE WALL

WHY: Thermal and acoustic insulation, camouflage of the living area, the noise of the rear wheels while driving and any other objects that we have insufficiently secured before driving, the constant noise of the refrigerator when parked (of course, if we decide to put it in the driver's cabin, which I highly recommend) – if these arguments are not appealing to you, you can skip this chapter.

HOW IT WORKS: The wall as one large element is cumbersome, and I can assure you that you will "walk through the wall" several times a day. In addition, the side door rail makes it difficult to put it on every time. That is why I decided to divide the wall into three elements: two small side "wings" and a "main wall". The side elements are installed permanently, which gives us a sense of privacy even when the main wall is removed – they cover the view from the front side windows, as well as slightly cover the front seats, which reduces the feeling of being in the car.

Mounting and opening the main wall can be done in several ways, but from experience I recommend the one that is the least troublesome and at the same time gives the most possibilities. The upper part of the wall is attached with magnets to the ceiling, and the lower part with magnets to the lower part of the wall that has not been cut out. The size of the main wall overlaps the "wings", so we are tight, but you can try a few magnets (each door closing causes air movement in the car, which, with too few magnets, may cause the wall to detach).

Thanks to fixing the wall with magnets, we can remove it completely and put it rolled up on the front seats or on the bed – where we are not residing at the moment. You can also, without unfastening its upper part, tilt it back and fix the lower part to the ceiling (also with magnets), because the acoustic foam wall is flexible enough. Magnets are a sensational invention that you will hear about here more than once! The detachable wall has one more additional use: if we just want to cover ourselves a little from the surroundings and noise in front, and at the same time: keep an eye on the outside situation, have better exchange of temperature and air throughout the car, or more light coming from the front windows, our great mobile wall can be placed on the front seats, leaning it against the backrests of the seats. This way, we will leave a clearance of several centimeters at the top.

MATERIALS:
- rubber foam: thickness 1 cm, density 50 kg / m³
- fabric (e.g. velor) with dimensions: 2 times the foam surface + 2 times its thickness
- glue (e.g. for upholstery or rubber, leather) – a lot!
- needle and thread
- acrylic double-sided adhesive tape: 1 cm wide, about 2 meters long
- neodymium magnets: 2 × 1.5 × 0.2 cm (50 pieces)

TOOLS:

* scissors, marker

HOW TO DO IT: First, place the armchairs and backrests in the furthest reclining position that you plan to use, because after making the wall, any pressure from the backrests will detach the wall from the fixing.

We start with the design: glue sheets of paper together and apply them to the side walls and the ceiling of the vehicle and trace the shape of our new wall (first "wings" and then the main wall). We cut out the shape from the sheet of paper and draw it on the foam rubber, which we can also easily cut with scissors. I recommend cutting out slightly larger pieces and trying them on regularly – you can always cut them more, but almost never stick them back (it will weaken the structure and add a lot of work). I also recommend leaving the main element of the wall far too large, because only at the end (after installing the "wings") it will become clear how exactly it fits to the whole and how much you need to cut.

Next we cover the perfectly matching "wings" with fabric (apart from some edges, but more on that in a moment). The acoustic foam is self-adhesive on one side, but I recommend using the same amount of glue on each side. Strong, elastic glue works perfectly in this case – be it in a spray (it spreads nicely) or in a liquid (it seems more efficient). You need to pay special attention to the adhesive part of the foam: once the material is applied there, it cannot be corrected (the foam will tear), so I do not recommend sticking the elements together by placing the foam on the material, but vice versa: on the foam lying on the ground, we put (unroll) the material and at the same time "iron" by hand or with a bar. If we do the opposite, we will not be able to see if the fabric underneath is wrinkling irretrievably. To increase durability, I recommend sewing the edges with a thread (a simple, wide seam every 1 cm is enough) – it is time-consuming, but at the same time it will add some elegance to the interior finish. Note: it's better to sew the edges if you won't be glueing the edges together, because it's very difficult to pierce the needle through the material that is stiff with dried glue.

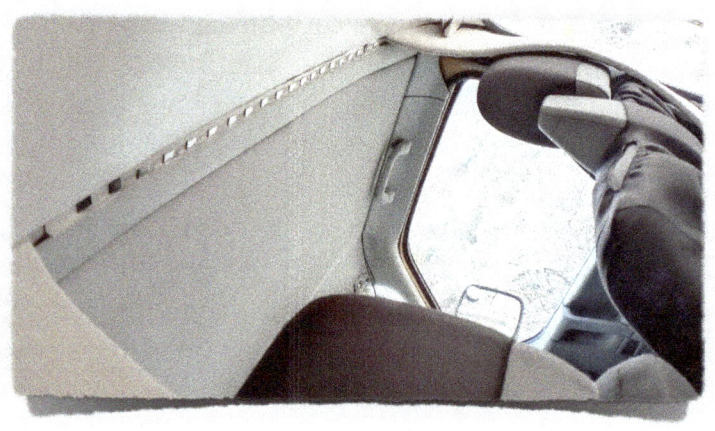

The right wing gracefully slides between the passenger seat and the side door rail.

After it's completely dry, glue the "wings" of the wall to the sides of the car. As it may be difficult and not durable to stick it directly to the car body, I suggest using an adhesive in the form of a double-sided acrylic tape (the thicker one), which is additionally covered with glue on each side. So it goes like this: when sticking the tape to the car, we additionally stick it with glue. Then we unlock the other side of the tape and smear it with glue as well, to put the "wings" of our wall against it at the very end. We hold it until we get bored and then let it dry.

The "wings" of our new wall.

Now it's time to finally try on the "middle" wall, cut it and then start upholstering it. Before wrapping it with fabric, we insert the magnets, which will be hidden under the fabric in order to protect them from possible detachment. We will use about 20 at the top (every 4-5 cm), about 5 at the bottom-front and about 15 at the bottom-rear – from the living area of the car. The latter will be used to attach the wall to the ceiling horizontally, i.e. "opening" the wall. At this stage, we don't have to worry about attaching them in the right place – we'll take care of it by installing magnets that attract them from the other side.

The easiest way to stick magnets to the foam is with our beloved double-sided tape (foam tears easily) and, if necessary, strengthen the connection with a few drops of glue. Then we cover the "main wall" with a fabric and sew it on – just like its "wings" before. After drying, we bring additional magnets closer to the upper edge so that they automatically pair with those under the fabric. We stick a strip of double-sided adhesive tape to the ceiling – exactly between the "wings". Finally, we attach our mobile wall to this very strip – this way we will stick the ceiling magnets exactly where they should be. Before this last step, it is worth adding a few drops of super glue to each ceiling magnet before applying them to the adhesive tape.

The lower magnets on the front of the wall will contact the metal part of the lower wall of the car that has not been cut out, so there is no need to stick additional magnets. On the other hand, mounting the ceiling magnets, that are used to hook the wall to the ceiling, is done almost similarly to those between the "wings".

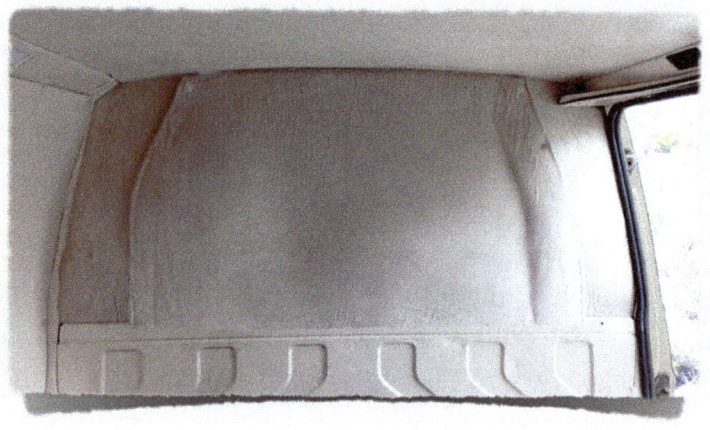

A mobile wall in all its glory.

4. WINDOW TO THE WORLD

TWO WINDOWS ARE BETTER THAN ONE

WHY: The size of the house in which we live (or rather its smallness) ceases to matter when we are surrounded by a vast, friendly surroundings. It compensates our senses for the few square meters of living space in our campervan. However, for all this to work so beautifully, we need to be able to see this space, and we don't always want to fully open the door (bad weather, noise, smell, etc.). Inserting a window in the side door will not only offer our eyes more space, but also give more light, which adds a lot of joy to our everyday life. The additional window will also allow you to park more easily or simply look around without having to go to the driver's cabin. Not to mention about stargazing at night while falling asleep.

WHAT WE NEED:
1. Side door glass (preferably new).
2. A visit to a garage specializing in car windows.

HOW TO DO IT: Personally, I only like to create a mess with wood filings, which is why I commissioned this task in a car repair shop. I also didn't want to worry about the tightness during every downpour, so I decided to outsource this task to professionals as the second and last one.

Sad door with no glass.

Happy glass door.

5. FLOOR

BEAUTIFUL IMPRESSION
WITH MINIMAL EFFORT

WHY: We will gain a bit more space by building the floor to the very edge of the car interior, and I'll even suggest covering a step at the side entrance door – the area beneath will still be available from the outside, e.g. to hide sneakers or flip-flops, which we won't have to look at while inside.

The floor can be made now or after the next chapter, in which we insert a fairly solid closet – then we'll be able to replace the floor elements without unscrewing the rather heavy closet. This sequence makes sense if we think long-term, and I can assure you that the floor will often be flooded, scratched or irretrievably soiled.

In my case, the car was already equipped with a one centimeter layer of plywood on the floor. However, it was not suitable for improvement, and besides, it did not increase the surface area in the way we'll be able to by installing an additional layer of flooring.

MATERIALS:
- plywood (e.g. coniferous), waterproof: 70 × 100 × 0.4 cm
- floor varnish (e.g. semi-matte)
- nails and/or wood screws

- aluminum profile: $2 \times 4 \times 100$ cm
- metal screws (4 pieces)

TOOLS:
- woodworking jigsaw
- handheld saw/wood circular saw (optional for your convenience)
- belt sander or orbital sander for wood
- hacksaw
- hammer and tapping tool (or screwdriver, if you prefer to use screws)

HOW TO DO IT: We start by mounting an additional support for the floor above the step (so we don't break it when stepping inside). In the existing old floor, we cut grooves for the aluminum profile and then screw it into the metal structure of the car (from what I was able to determine, the car has a double layer there, so we won't make a hole right through).

A floor without THE floor.

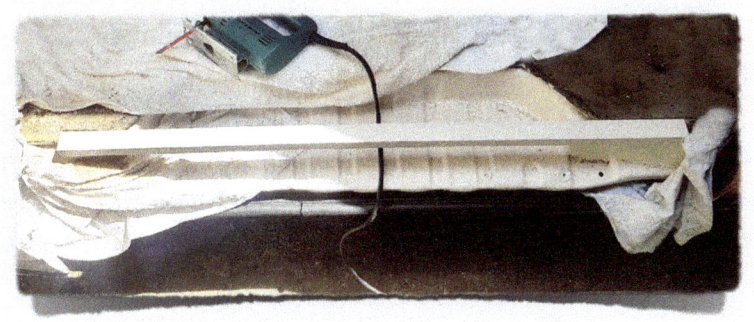

Aluminum bracket, thanks to which we'll gain up to...
0.15 m² of living space!

Then we make the floor itself: stick the sheets of paper together with tape and put them around the interior of the car, trace the shape of all the elements, cut out and trace them one by one on the pieces of plywood. As always, I recommend cutting out slightly larger shapes and testing them repeatedly, even after the smallest correction. Note:

A floor with an extra layer of flooring.

plywood likes to "tear" during cutting – to prevent this, we cut the outline with a bookbinding knife (thanks G.K. for the good advice!).

We try on all ready-made elements at once and, without changing their position, nail them one by one. I suggest using small nails with a flat head – they look more aesthetically pleasing than screws. Over time, it may turn out that in some places you will have to replace the nail with a small screw – you can pour resin glue over it.

After all the floor elements are installed, we gently knock down the nails. The plywood is thin, so it needs to be done very delicately, but it's definitely worth giving you the comfort of not hooking on the protruding heads of nails.

We feed the fully fixed floor with a super-strong floor varnish – first once, and after several hours for a second time. We don't regret the amount – we will thank ourselves for it after every accidental spill of a drink, dirt or scratching the floor by accidentally dropping sharp object during everyday use.

6. CABINET

A MAGIC CABINET
FOR EVERYTHING YOU NEED TO LIVE

WHY: The cabinet is our center for meeting the needs of everyday life. It's special because it also supplies us with water and electricity. Therefore, it cannot be an ordinary cupboard. It has to be a very solid, real cabinet. It does not reach the ceiling for better ventilation and access to the water tank (it's easier to unscrew and tighten it before driving). The doors to the shelves do not fully cover them, ensuring air exchange – in a closed car it can get really hot, and the shelves adjacent to the heated walls will get the most heat. Additionally, we have an initial insight into what's on each shelf. And why the door to the shelves at all, if the front bars already protect items from falling out? At least in my opinion, looking at the contents of the shelves every day is not a very thrilling sight – I definitely prefer looking at wood that is more pleasing to the eye.

The depth of the cabinet suggested here takes into account the width of the bed (90 cm) and the distance between them (10 cm). Thanks to this small space we'll be able to see and even modify something in our small "power plant" located in the lowest shelf. This space also makes it easier to lift the bed to reach the load stored underneath it.

In addition, accidentally splashing water from the sink will land on this small piece of floor, and not on the mattress on which we sleep or sit during the day. You just need to think about a wedge between the cabinet and the bed, otherwise after every ride with even one sharp turn to the left, our bed will move a bit to the right and you'll have to manually move it back to its place (with all its contents). It is important that the wedge rests against a solid cabinet wall rather than against a less solid sink cabinet (more about it in the next chapter).

The depth of the cabinet also takes into account the location of our "recreational" battery placed parallel to the wheel arch. It can also be mounted behind the wheel arch, i.e. perpendicular to the side wall of the wardrobe, provided that its distance from the rear door of the car is properly planned. Therefore, already at this stage you have to decide on a specific solution for supplying power in your campervan, e.g. on the dimensions of the battery, or simply take this dimension into account in the event that you decide to use such a battery later.

MATERIALS:
- wood boards (2 cm thick, preferably waterproof):
  ❖ 2 on the sides: 36 × 125 cm
  ❖ 4 placed horizontally: 36 × 90 cm
  ❖ 5 at the front of each shelf: 5 × 90 cm (prevent items from falling out even with open doors)
  ❖ 3 front doors: 11 × 90 cm (three shelves will have doors with hinged mounting)
  ❖ 1 front panel for lowest compartment: 23 × 90 cm (removable – here will be our little "power plant")
- screws (6 mm × 0.4 cm) – for fixing boards

• metal brackets (15 × 3 × 0.5 cm, 4 pcs.) – for fixing the cabinet to the wall of the car

• screws (4 × 0.6 cm) and nuts (12 pcs.) – for screwing the cabinet with metal brackets to the car wall

• hinges (2 cm wide, 6 pcs.) – for opening the shelves

• flat head nails (24 pcs.) – for fixing the hinges

• magnets (6 pcs.) and small metal plates (6 pcs. – to close the door to each shelf)

• hooks (2 or 4 pcs.) attach the lower door of the "power plant"

• wood varnish

TOOLS:
• circular saw or miter saw
• belt sander and/or orbital sander for wood

HOW TO DO IT: At the beginning, we set the height of each shelf: at least one must be high enough to comfortably fit the highest item on it that we plan to hide there (e.g. a large jar) – let's add a few centimeters for the operation of removing the item, i.e. slightly tilting it to avoid the front bar protecting against falling out of objects. I divided the top shelf in half to make room for a running water tank (more on this in the next chapter). The lowest shelf is high enough to fit the battery in it and leave a few centimeters for the top and bottom ventilation. Ultimately, the heights of the shelves are as follows (from bottom to top):

• lower: 28 cm (for "power plant")
• three middle ones: 22, 20, 18 cm (any order)
• upper (without doors, divided in half): 36 cm
  ❖ left side: 36 cm (for a water tank)
  ❖ right side divided into two: 18 cm, 18 cm

A magical cabinet in all its glory.

The side boards must be given a curvature corresponding to the curvature of the side wall of the car. Then we screw them with the horizontal boards, then the front boards, and and finally we mount the doors of each wardrobe. Of course, magnets will work great here – one on each side of the door. From the side of the cabinet I recommend installing a piece of thin metal – using another magnet here may make it difficult to open the cabinet door, and in addition, too much force from the magnets may tear them out of the fixing. Everything can be mounted with double-sided adhesive tape with the addition of super glue (I always recommend the "gel" version of the instant glue – everything vibrates in the car while driving, and the gel works better in such conditions). Additionally, deep inside each shelf, at the bottom, we can attach two-centimeter high bars to prevent objects from falling onto the wall. The wall of the car is inclined inwards, so objects falling on it may tilt and, consequently, fall over or "fly" onto the objects in front of them. I recommend installing the same bars at the very bottom of the cabinet, but in a slightly different amount and for a different purpose: we install two bars on which the battery will stand and whatever else we wish to mount there. This will increase the ventilation of the devices from the bottom and most importantly: it will prevent possible flooding in the event of an unexpected "flood" (spilled drink, changing the gray water tank, etc.). Ultimately, we attach the cabinet to the car wall with at least two solid metal brackets (i.e. thick pieces of metal) and screws – this is a very important step.

*The cabinet is closed by the miraculous force
of magnetic attraction.*

An accidental use for one of the cabinet doors.

7. SINK + WATER + STOVE

NO PUMP, JUST PURE FORCE OF GRAVITY

WHY: Lack of sink, that is, pouring water "overboard" means splashing in the mud all your life, or at least the entire camper van live. In addition, the weather does not always encourage you to wash parts of your body or wash dishes outside, and especially to look for a place where you can do it in a way that is harmless to yourself and the environment. Therefore, we'll build a very small cabinet that will fit half the kitchen, i.e.: a sink, a gray water tank, and even a stove and a trash can.

HOW IT WORKS: The most popular law of physics, which is gravity, will let the water flow from the tank on the top of the cabinet down towards the sink, and from there straight to the gray water tank – right under the sink. We fill and empty the tanks in the right places on the world map, and the more we take them with us, the longer we'll stay in our favorite place without having to refill and empty them (I suggest at least two gray water tanks and two clean ones – one with a tap and one without it), and I can assure you that the constant search for such places can make everyday life quite unpleasant. After each change, it is worth pouring a solid tablespoon of baking soda into the gray water tank. Vinegar is best for periodic rinsing.

WHAT WE NEED:

1. Water tank: 20 liters with a tap and a vent at the top (absolutely necessary!) + tap-on hose + hose end (optional for greater hose stability and great visual appearance – strongly recommended).

2. Gray water tank: 20 liters, preferably also with an air vent (greatly facilitates emptying – the tank does not "choke", so it does not splash).

3. Sink (without siphon): 45 × 30 × 15 cm.

4. Connector screwed to the sink drain (instead of a siphon), and on the other side ended with a narrow funnel/drain – one that will fit into the opening of the gray water tank (about 3 cm in diameter).

5. Wood boards for the sink cabinet frame (2 cm thick, 4 cm wide):
   - legs: 54.5 cm long (4 or 5 pieces – e.g. in my van, the side wall of the car has a recess for the door in the middle, so we need 5 legs)
   - horizontal supports for the cabinet top, lengths: 55 cm (2 pieces) and 35 cm (2 pieces)
   - waterproof plywood for the walls of the cabinet:
   - front and back: 54,5 cm × 59 cm (2 pieces)
   - side (the door of the cabinet): 31 cm × 58 cm
   - top: 35 cm × 54 cm.

6. Wood varnish.

7. Nails and screws.

8. Angles for stiffening the cabinet structure.

TOOLS:

- woodworking jigsaw
- handheld saw/circular saw for wood (optional for your convenience)

- belt sander or orbital sander for wood
- screwdriver and/or hammer (if using nails)

HOW TO DO IT: We place the water tank with the tap on the upper shelf of our solid cabinet by the left wall (placing it there will give you another advantage, but more on that in the chapter on... lighting). On the same wall of the same cabinet, we cut an opening through which the entire tap will protrude. Attaching a hose to the tap will let the water flow gracefully towards the sink. It's a good idea to cut a little more at the bottom of the hole and consider installing the tank slightly at an angle to use as much water from the tank as possible – the tap is mounted at a certain height in the tank, preventing the full use of the water. For this purpose, the shelf with the tank should be provided with an additional piece of wood, which will cause the water tank to be in a slightly oblique position. We fill the remaining area behind the tank with something that will immobilize it while driving, e.g. with our favorite hammock. To protect the tank from falling to the side, we secure it with a relatively easily detachable crossbar, e.g. with a bamboo stick locked in metal hooks, which we screw into the cabinet – on both sides of the tank.

How to plan the construction of the sink? On the outside of the cabinet, on the left, place the gray water tank on the floor. Place a sink on the tank, with the drain already screwed on, aimed straight at the center of the tank inlet. Bearing in mind this course of events, we plan the dimensions of the cabinet.

Additionally, the following must be taken into account at this point:

• 1-2 cm of clearance between the sink outlet and the gray water tank inlet (the sink should not rest on the tank, but on the cabinet), so ultimately the sink will be 1-2 cm higher

• about 20-22 cm of space on the left side for the gas tank with a stove (Polish and, for example, a Spanish cylinder weighing about 2 kg is exactly the same diameter), which will be closed in the cabinet while driving

• about 1-2 cm for the "wedge" to prevent the gas tank and gray water tank from "dancing" in the cabinet while driving. I recommend fastening the door to the cabinet with the use of magnets (it has a lot of advantages, which I will mention in a moment), so it is necessary to securely immobilize the tanks.

Cabinet frame with five legs
(the fifth is shy – it hid around the corner).

The above-mentioned 1-2 centimeters of clearance between the sink outlet and the gray water tank inlet have one big advantage, one small advantage and one medium-sized disadvantage. The sink loosely placed above the tank can be "leveled" a bit after parking on uneven ground, which prevents the unpleasant view of standing water in the sink (in the case of a flat sink bottom, which we'll most probably buy because it's the most capacious one). It's also easy to remove the sink when replacing the gray water tank, which will take place every few days. The disadvantage of this solution is, unfortunately, leakage in the case of high levels of gray water and large unevenness on the road. The solution (a bit troublesome) is removing the sink and closing the tank before driving with the alarm level of gray water (over 3/4 full).

Gravity sewage system.

It is worth considering a tight connection, e.g. in the form of a rubber hose connecting the sink outlet with the tank inlet – a flexible connection is necessary due to the car's vibrations while driving, as well as the possibility of "leveling" the sink on an uneven parking spot. For this purpose, you can cut a hole in the cap from the tank, thread a rubber hose through it and seal it. From the side of the sink, you can do something similar: connect the upper end of the pipe tightly to the nut that will be screwed onto the threaded end of the sink drain. Then we screw the pipe to the gray water tank and to the drain with a simultaneous rotating movement. Certainly, the tank cap must tighten to the end, but at the top it does not seem so important, so the threads (at the top and bottom) do not have to be of the same length.

It is best to equip the cabinet door with magnets (3 on each side: on the door and in the cabinet), and if we mount them close to the side edges, we'll be able to open them to each side – depending on our needs. When we decide to use hinges, we have to prepare for the dilemma: from which side should we mount them? The universal solution with magnets gives us two more great amenities: we can completely get rid of the door and conveniently replace the gray water tank, as well as tilt it sideways (towards the open side door of the car) serving as a wind shield when using the stove.

I recommend that you make a rubbish bin in a flexible version, that is: put less elegant bags (or used food packaging) into an elegant paper bag shaped like a basket with a flat bottom. Even a 5-kilogram package of baking soda will fit there, which is enough for a year of travel.

Gravitational "water supply" system.

The rubber hose attached to the tap of our clean water tank can be terminated with an elegant tip (one of those attached to a garden hose). It's also a good idea to mount a holder to the side wall of the cabinet that will prevent the hose from "swinging" while driving. It'll also stabilize the source of flowing water while washing dishes, and if necessary, it will allow for completely free manipulation of the entire hose. I recommend installing the tip of the hose as low as possible (even 5–7 cm from the top edge of the sink) and getting used to using the water low in the sink, rather than having the water constantly splash on the countertop. If we attach the end of the hose with the handle closer to the wall of the cabinet, then with controlled movements we'll even be able to wash our head in the sink without splashing the entire surroundings too much.

Both tanks blocked with a simple hatch
– the cabinet is packed for the road.

We use the metal bracket that fastens the big cabinet to the wall as a hanger for cutlery. At first it felt a bit too posh, but when I tried it myself, I never stopped, and even started to hang a lighter on it to start the stove. You can buy a special magnetic strip or go for a more economical version and use the magnets that we've already been using for many other things.

The wedge in the form of a wooden board blocking the gas tank and the gray water tank is perfect for tilting the van's hatch for extra ventilation. This can be done in two ways: slightly or wider depending on which side of the board we use. Multifunctionality is the most desirable feature of any item that we plan to use in such a small space.

The cabinet door is a great protection against the wind.

UPDATE (OCTOBER 2023):

As soon as I came across a small USB-charged water pump online, I couldn't resist its functionality as well as minimalist design. Moreover, it turned out to solve two problems: not using the full capacity of the water tank because of the faucet mounted too high, as well as the noise of ostentatiously splashing water in the tank due to its mounting high on the cabinet. When driving on uneven surfaces, the splashing noise can be felt!

If you decide on a water pump at the very beginning, then when building a cabinet with a sink you need take into account the dimensions of the two tanks. In my case there was a modification, so I had to gain the missing 1.5 centimeters by creating a frame for the door closing the cabinet. Since the door is fixed with magnets, we need to additionally secure the

Sewage system: version with a minimalist water pump.

clean water tank so that it does not come out of the cabinet during, for example, sharp braking. This can be done with two wedges, as in the attached picture. One long wedge blocks the tank from bouncing. The second cube-shaped one is wedged between the first one and the tank carrying handle.

Water pump stand with a hole for a rubber hose.

Then we make a wooden stand/holder that matches the diameter of the pump we have purchased and drill a hole in it. Through this hole, we can run a rubber hose for clean water from under the sink. We can easily get such hose in any decent construction store. It is worth protecting the stand well with varnish for obvious reasons. Next we insert the other end of the hose into the clean water tank in one of two ways:

1) through a hole drilled in the cap (watch out: sealing it will prevent necessary air exchange)

2) through a special nut, which is also a tap, and through which the rubber hose can be squeezed (see: previous photo).

These types of pumps are not expensive, so I recommend buying a spare one right away – we'll avoid unnecessary trouble in the event of a possible failure of the water system in the middle of the trip.

USB-charged minimalist pump in action.

8. ELECTRICITY

SOLAR PANEL, CONTROLLER AND BATTERY – "HOLY TRINITY" FOR EVERYONE?

WHY: It all depends on our needs. If we plan to use electricity to do something more than just charge a phone, and we don't want to play around with setting up a so-called mobile "power station", which involves taking the equipment out of the van for the time of charging, keeping an eye on it and putting it back before each ride, we need a solid system that will keep working – without bothering us every day. The "power station" is a small, mobile, ready-to-use device, but at the same time a very expensive "all-in-one" device (panel + controller + inverter + battery) – good fun for short trips, but not, for example, for half a year of travel. Hanging out in cafes just to recharge your devices? You have to like to hang out in cafes a lot. Or maybe the battery itself and charging it somewhere once a week? This is also an option that may be completely sufficient for some people. Either way, it is worth considering a fully independent option.

HOW IT WORKS: A solar panel (photovoltaic – PV for short) installed on the roof of a van draws energy from the sun, which we can use on an ongoing basis and/or store it

41

in a battery. Even on a cloudy day, a sufficiently large panel can provide energy for current needs (e.g. a 280 watt panel will provide about 50 watts, and this is enough to power a typical travel refrigerator; another interesting fact: during a rainstorm it will provide 25 watts). Electricity for current needs, as well as any surplus that we want to transfer to the battery, must be passed through the so-called controller/converter that, among other things, will convert the voltage coming from the panels (e.g. 31 volts) to the amount that our devices like (about 12 V), or a battery (about 13-14 V). And how much of this electricity do our devices need? This value is usually given by manufacturers in amperes (A) or watts (W), and that's all we need to remember from elementary school physics lessons. The only formula that interests us here is the one for power! Without unnecessarily going into specialized nomenclature, it actually looks really nice:

$$\text{power (W)} = \text{voltage (V)} \times \text{current (A)}$$

(W – watt, V – volt, A – ampere)

For example: if the manufacturer of the most ordinary travel refrigerator says that it uses 4 amps and runs on about 12.5 volts, we already know that it needs 50 watts of power ($12.5 \times 4 = 50$). The manufacturer may also give the same information, but differently: 50 watts and 12.5 volts. Then we twist the formula a bit and we get the same, i.e. 4 amps (50 W = 12.5 V × intensity, so intensity is: 50 W / 12.5 V) -- for each hour of device operation! So in 10 hours, such a refrigerator will consume 40 amperes of electricity. Therefore we need 4 amps × 24 hours, which is 96 ampere hours (Ah for short) to keep it running around the clock.

The solar panel does not provide us with as much electricity as it can during most of the sunny day – keep this in mind when thinking about buying, for example, a 100 watt panel, which will only be enough to charge a laptop and a mobile phone every day. This is the peak value that the panel can reach when the sun is at its zenith, so be prepared to get half the power offered on a sunny day on average. One large panel means less cables, less assembly work and less philosophising about whether it is better to connect them in series or in parallel. The only advantage of having several panels is the ability to use the others in the event of failure of one of them – I took the risk and... I got myself an emergency 230 V charger.

The panel is mounted with the use of handles that distance our panel from the roof, allowing for air exchange (an excessively heated panel reduces its efficiency), and on the other hand, it creates a not necessarily favorable air duct, which fortunately can be easily eliminated by mounting the fairing.

The controller, in addition to the already known skill of changing the voltage of the current flowing through it, will also make the best use of photovoltaic cells, as well as maintain the health of our leisure battery. The best controller is the new type MPPT (the older ones are PWM) and it is not worth saving here, because in fact it will be the other way around: we will use up our battery faster (MPPT have special algorithms, e.g. regulating the amount of charging voltage depending on the battery charge level), slower will be charged (MPPT are 30% more efficient than PWM), so we will be unnecessarily looking for bigger solar panels, higher battery capacity or simply replacing the battery more often.

The same applies to **the battery**: the "gel" (lead-acid) battery is cheaper, but many physics experts have already proved that we'll incur a much higher cost over the years (more frequent replacement) than when buying a much more expensive lithium-ion (Li-Ion) battery, and even better lithium-iron-phosphate (LiFePO4), which I recommend most – not only because of the lower risk of failure (e.g. explosion), but also longer service life. However, you have to take into account the fact that it can absolutely never be charged at temperatures below 0°C, as we will damage it immediately. Therefore, you must either maintain a constant positive temperature in our small power plant, or disconnect it from the charger (i.e. from the controller) while staying in negative temperatures.

If you don't plan such luxuries as a fridge or electric heating, and for example consider using only a laptop, then you can consider buying only a battery and a charger. Then every 5-7 days or so connect to an ordinary 230 V socket somewhere (similarly: a charger with a charging power of 10 amps will charge a battery with a capacity of 100 Ah in 10 hours). You can also buy a solar panel itself and a simple controller with USB outputs that will charge with the current available at the moment – good enough to charge a mobile phone, but to charge a laptop in such a variable and unpredictable cycle, I wouldn't risk the health of its battery. A big power bank (e.g. 20,000 mAh = 20 Ah) that can provide enough amps to charge your laptop is also an interesting alternative.

An additional idea for charging the battery is a sensible connection to the car's alternator, i.e. using an intelligent splitter that will share the current only when the alternator is generous enough at the moment (factory-installed alternators are not designed to withstand higher loads).

Wait a minute, how is it going to work with our devices? Here we have twelve volts, and a typical laptop or our favorite sonic toothbrush works with a 110 or 230 V power supply ?! Nothing could be more wrong. This power supply is used to reduce the voltage from 110/230 V to, for example, 12 or 5 volts. If we are ready to abandon our favorite curling iron, blender or any other gadget that requires 110/230 V, we will save the world a lot of unnecessary energy conversion, and our battery life will be significantly extended. If we search well, we'll find a laptop that we can charge via the USB-C port, as well as a 30 W charger with a car socket. The brush is also available with a charging cable in the most popular USB version, that is USB-A, which can be connected to any car phone charger. In this way, we get rid of the additional cost and labor associated with the purchase of an inverter, which would of course be another source of noise (it needs a fan to cool itself). If, however, we find that the pop curls on our head are an indispensable part of our personality, then this inverter can be purchased, but treated as an additional power source --only for special occasions.

Ultimately, all we need to do now is to count how many ampere hours we need to be happy during our camper van life, taking into account:

• weather factors (e.g. number of hours of sunshine per day, possible lack of sun for several days)

- strategy of using devices (e.g. turning off the refrigerator at night – we'll surely eat everything in a few days
before it starts to rot, and we'll sleep without noise next
to our ears)
- destination (e.g. it's cold in the mountains, so the
refrigerator doesn't have to work, but the heating does).

The following proposal of building our small "power plant"
is enough for: using a tourist refrigerator for about 12 to
14 hours a day, charging a laptop and one or two mobile
phones (a laptop or a mobile phone is almost a negligible
power consumption compared to a refrigerator or heating)
– in a place where the sun shines for at least 8 hours a day
and you may end up with a day or two in a row without
any sun. The latter factor determines the purchase of
almost twice as much battery capacity as needed, and some
spare is always worth having.

WHAT WE NEED:
   1. Solar panel (PV): 280 W, 34 V (at least 200 W or
2 × 100 W), for example with dimensions of 120 ×
100 × 70 cm, a tempered glass coating – the same is
mounted on the roofs of buildings. When buying
a panel, remember to add the width of the dimensions
of the mounting brackets.
   2. Solar panel mounting brackets: length 8 cm,
height 3 cm, width 3 cm, thickness 2 mm (4 pieces in
the case of a 100-150 watt panel, and for larger panels,
I recommend 6-8 pieces and cut the so-called fairing
from the sheet of metal, so that the air stream blowing
under the PV won't make it fly away) + bolts, nuts,
washers.

3. Rubber (e.g. EPDM): thickness min. 3 mm, density 1.5 g/cm³, resistant to water, UV, resistant to aging in weather conditions (to put under the entire surface of the mounting brackets for solar panels, as well as a possible fairing – it will seal and slightly dampen vibrations).

4. PG7 cable gland for a cable with a diameter of 4 mm (I recommend going crazy and buying stainless steel version, because it's still a penny expense), IP68 protection class, resistant to external temperatures (2 pieces – for safe and tight passage of cables going from the solar panel to the interior of the car).

5. MPPT Solar Charge Controller, e.g. "100 V, 20 A" or at least "75 V, 15 A" (preferably with Bluetooth communication). The first parameter tells us that the controller can accept a maximum current of 100 volts from solar panels (e.g. if we connect two 100 watt 12 V panels in series, the controller must be ready to accept 24 V. Another example is a 280 watt panel. which produces a voltage in the range of 31-36 volts. The second given value, expressed in amperes, is the maximum current that the controller is able to transmit to our devices and the battery (even if the panels produce more of it) – of course after changing the voltage to 12 V (for devices) and 13-14 V (for battery charging).

6. LiFePO4 battery: nominal voltage 12.8 V, nominal capacity 100 Ah, maximum discharge current 100 A (maximum current that is available at the moment), maintenance-free with built-in BMS (battery man-agement system).

7. Fuse block/fuse panel (12V) distributes the current for our devices, additionally securing each of them with a separate (car) fuse, preferably with negative bus (if it lacks earthing connectors, then we need to buy a separate grounding strip – see below) + fuses for each device (with an amperage of approx. 25–30% more than the device needs to operate).

8. Negative bus bar/terminal block (if our fuse block does not have one – see above), i.e. a piece of copper with holes for negative wires that will ground each of our devices.

9. Fuse holder or circuit breaker (12 V) will be used in three or at least two places: between the PV and the controller, between the controller and the battery, and optionally between the battery and the fuse panel. They will protect our devices from overcurrent, allow us to turn off a part or the whole system when we are not using the campervan or when we want to repair something. It's also the first step in extinguishing any fire.

10. Car/marine socket/power outlet (12 V): threaded for convenient mounting in the walls; maximum power 240 W (20 A) – it may seem too careful (and you can't be too careful), but I recommend installing a separate socket for each device that consumes serious amounts of power, (i.e. 3 amperes up) – they get really warm after a few hours, so it's worth separating this heat for devices like refrigerators, heating blankets or even laptops. The only downside of such sockets is that the springs inside some of the plugs are too strong and they easily "pop out" (this can sometimes be corrected by disassembling the plug) – even though the sockets have a so-called "lock point", which is supposed to keep the plug in the socket.

11. Cables and connectors:

• Copper PV cable: 4 mm² (enough to transmit up to 12 amps with a maximum length of 5 m), resistant to UV radiation and other weather conditions (because it will be outside the car) + MC4 connectors to extend the factory-installed cables in the solar panel (2 male and 2 female).

• Copper stranded cable: 1.5 mm² cross-section (will transmit max. 4.5 A). It is most convenient to buy a two-core cable right away, which means having two wires in one cable that will cover the current and grounding) – in solid insulation, and length to be counted later on.

• Copper stranded cable: 16 mm² cross-section (will transmit max. 48 A) – in solid insulation.

• Ring terminal connectors: width 6.3 mm, insulated (at least 4 pieces for a 16 mm² wire and 1 piece for a 1.5 mm² wire) – for connecting the cables to the leisure battery.

• Flat female connector for a 1.5 mm² cable, insulated – for connecting devices with a fuse panel equipped with male connectors (at least one for each 12 V device or socket that we plan to supply with electricity), and if the negative bus bar or the device also has male connectors, we buy an adequately larger number of female ones.

12. Crimping tool may seem like quite an expense, but it will save us a lot of trouble and uncertainty when crimping cables in connectors or removing insulation from cables.

HOW TO DO IT: Let's not panic looking at the diagrams below, because they are governed by only two very simple rules:

1. We connect plus to plus, and minus to minus (the exception is serial connection of solar panels or batteries, but in our "minimal" version we do not bother with such solutions).

2. The thickness of the copper wire (colloquially "cable", although the cable may contain several wires; also: the thickness of the cable includes the thickness of the insulation) – appropriate for the current it transmits and the temperature of its location (we use slightly thicker wires at higher temperatures – the thicker, the less chance it will heat up, melt and cause a fire).

Of course, we use "stranded" type cables, those which, instead of one thick wire, have many thin, flexible wires inside the insulation. Such cables can be bent almost infinitely without compromising their health, which is very important in the case of a car that vibrates while driving, as well as during any modifications to our system. The greater the number of strands, the better contact of the wire with the socket. A good 1.5 mm² wire should have at least 30 strands inside the insulation.

In case of a campervan, the thickness of the cables, which can reach temperatures of up to 40°C inside, is limited to two types (we always talk about the cross-sectional area of the copper wire inside – without any layers of insulation):

1. Current up to 15 A = 1.5 mm² cable
2. Current up to 100 A = 16 mm² cable

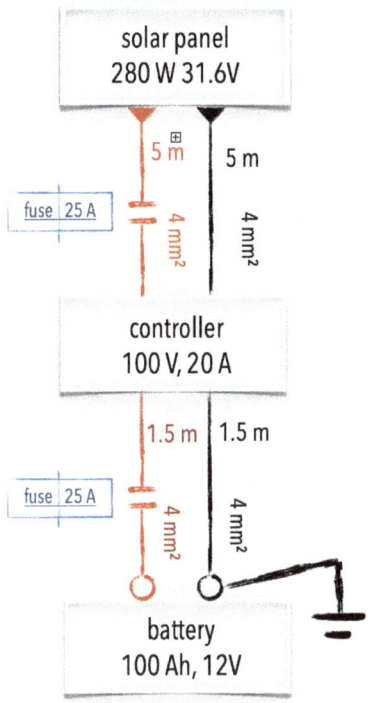

Connection diagram of our "Electric Holy Trinity".

The diagram seems to get very complicated when we add our devices to it, but I can assure you that it is only an optical illusion...

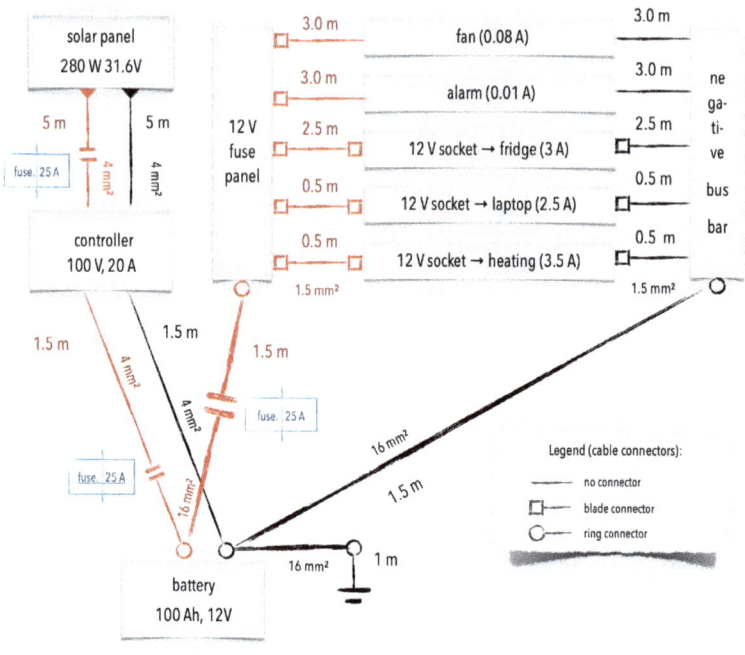

Diagram of connection of the entire power plant in the "minimal" version, that is: 1 panel → 1 controller → 1 battery

After drawing the diagram for your own energy needs (or reworking the following one) – the planning phase – we go to the supply phase:

1. We measure the surface of our power plant to know the size of the devices we can fit there, bearing in mind the requirements of their operating conditions (e.g. a more powerful controller requires better cooling – more distance from the walls).

2. We buy all the necessary equipment in order to plan the arrangement in our small power plant (for the convenience of operation, and above all, to maintain a safety distance).

3. We measure the distances between devices to plan the cable lengths and list the types of connectors that our devices require.

4. With our shopping list, we go to the electrical store, where (optionally), under the watchful eye of a professional, we confirm ourselves in our intentions (with questions such as: will this switch work with so many amps, etc.).

Finally, we move on to the most interesting phase, which is: the implementation phase. Very important: in the end, we connect all the cables in the reverse order than the course of events described here (which in practice will boil down to plugging in a few fuses and turning one switch, if we decide to use it). The sequence kept here is to make it easier to understand the idea of the whole system:

1. **The solar panel** already has cables, usually terminated with the MC4 connectors, so for assembly purposes we need to get rid of them – first by trying to disassemble them (unscrew the back cap and try to pull the cable out of the connector using some force) and if this won't work, we need to cut them off and use new connectors (to extend the cable) – of course after pulling the cables inside the car. We secure the ends of the extension cables, because the panel exposed to the sun is already doing its job conscientiously, and we don't need any accidental short circuit (by the way, experiencing the voltage from 30 V is quite unpleasant).

You can also cover the PV from the sun, for example with a piece cardboard, which, by the way, will protect it against an accidental impact of a passing tool. At both ends of each cable, I recommend wrapping a piece of tape with a description of the source and the purpose of the cable end, e.g. "PV (+) → MPPT (+)", or at least with the symbol "+" or "−", which will save us solving many unnecessary puzzles while connecting the whole system and any possible servicing.

An alternative solution is buying a dual cable entry gland – a piece of plastic in perfectly white color that we have to stick to the roof, which I consider an unnecessary entertainment, because holes in the roof will have to be drilled anyway.

Next we put the solar panel on the roof of the car and make sure that it's the perfect place for it and that moving it by 1 cm one way or the other will not be better. For this purpose, we remove the ceiling panels inside the car and check whether we have access to screwing the handles in a given place (for example, a few "ribs" pass across the roof of my van, strengthening the structure, but effectively hindering the installation of the solar panel). The roof may also have a curvature along the length of the car, which means that moving the panel forward and backward will change its angle of inclination in relation to the air flow that develops while driving. The excess pressure generated under the panel is unlikely to cause us to start flying, but for a better ride comfort, it can be eliminated in a simple way by installing a piece of cover (e.g. made of a piece of metal) on the entire width of the PV, directing this air stream over the panel.

Panel with fairing ready for road surfing.

There are also plastic mounting brackets for solar panels, which do not require drilling, but gluing. Such handles can be a great inspiration for nightmares about a solar panel taking off while driving, so apart from the undisputed matter of your own taste in terms of color and material used, they can be used only for small panels of 100 W. However, you have to pay at least three times more for it than for a set of metal brackets.

It may also be tempting to screw the solar panel directly to the roof (I saw such a case with my own eyes and that PV surely had more than 300 W!). It didn't seem quite as crazy as it looked, as due to the curvature of the roof, ventilation and drainage could take place. In such case the temptation of our panel to "take off" seems averted and our camper van becomes a bit more stealthy. However, I can't really tell how the lack of proper ventilation under the PV affects its efficiency.

Going back to our plan: we synchronize the perfectly planned location of the PV with the equally ideally located mounting brackets, which we'll eventually have to bend slightly due to the second curvature of the roof, which runs across it. The PV frame already has some mounting holes, but it may turn out that we need to carefully drill new ones.

Next we screw the brackets to the PV with the support of solid washers and cut pieces of durable rubber that will cover the area between the roof and each bracket. This way we'll prevent the accumulation of moisture underneath as well as absorb some vibrations, because everyone deserves some driving comfort – even our shiny solar panel.

We can now decide to drill two holes for the PV wires (which, hidden under the panel, will pass through the car roof with the help of cable glands) or at least determine their exact location – not too far from the edge of the panel, so that when tightening the glands we can reach them with a flat screwdriver. Without PV on the roof, drilled holes are now easier to grind with a half-round file, which will allow for safer and smoother insertion of cables.

Finally, we put our PV on the roof, mark the location of its mounting brackets (e.g. with painter's tape) and measure the distance from the edge on both sides of the car so that the panel is aimed as much as possible to the direction of driving straight ahead. Then we cross all our fingers, hold our breath and... drill boldly into the roof – preferably already with rubber placed under each bracket. Next we cross our fingers even more and, still holding our breath, we look inside the car, to make sure that the hole is in our dream place, that is where we can reach it with the key to tighten each nut. In order to help our dreams come true, you can first drill very small holes, which in case of a mistake will be easier to forget about (e.g. by gluing it without leaving too much trace). To avoid constantly adjusting the position of the solar panel, you can start by screwing it onto the opposite ends of PV.

Cable glands sitting safely under the "roof". PV frame and mounting brackets are camouflaged with matt foil.

After successfully tightening all the screws, it's time for the fairing, that is a piece of flexible, yet solid sheet of metal, which at the bottom is screwed to the roof along the front side of the PV's frame, and its remaining part is bent upwards, so that it finally rests on the front side of the frame. Due to the curvature of the roof, screwing on this piece of metal is not that easy as we have to bend it slightly. Therefore, it is worth drilling the mounting holes both in the roof and in the fairing at the same time when the element is finally bent. Under the fairing, along its entire length, a rubber mat (i.e. a seal) is also very welcome.

The PV cables, that we've led inside the car can be

extended with additional connectors and an additional amount of solar cable. Then we hide them nicely behind the panels covering the ceiling and walls of our camper van, so that the ends of the cables stick out close to our destination...

2. The controller should be mounted in accordance with the manufacturer's recommendations, i.e. in a vertical position and at a distance of at least 10-15 cm from each side – except, of course, the wall to which it will be attached. For this purpose, you can add a piece of plywood between the floor and the first lower shelf of our cabinet and screw to it our wonderfully exposed controller, as well as both fuse sockets, which can be easily reached in case of a more or less urgent need.

The solar cable with the minus, which we conscientiously and responsibly marked with a tape with the inscription "-", is connected directly to the "-" socket in the controller in the PV section. Whereas the "+" cable is first cut (around 15 cm near its end) in order to install the fuse holder and eventually connected to the "PV +" socket of the controller. It is also worth putting some effort to the correct placement of the cables in the sockets: we make sure to put a maximum length of uninsulated cable into the socket, and at the same time don't leave the "naked" part outside, as it may accidentally come into contact with other uninsulated cables.

3. The battery, although it already has a casing that serves a protective function, can additionally be put on something, which will prevent possible contact with any unexpected liquids that may flow through our floor (completely by accident, of course). In addition, we'll provide ventilation from the bottom, if we mount two wooden slats along the lowest shelf of the cabinet, which will form a kind of "rails", and to which you can additionally attach anything else you want (eg the previously mentioned inverter). It's best to assume in advance that everything inside the campervan can one day travel in every possible direction in space, so even something as heavy as a battery should be immobilized.

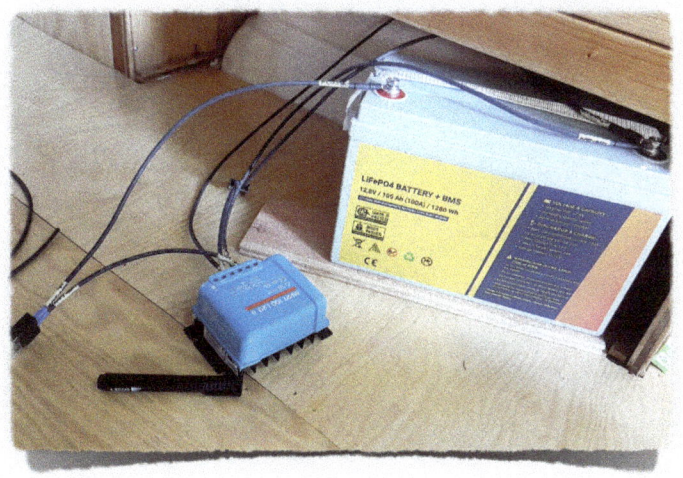

The controller blinks, which means it's alive, and that means it's ready to be mounted in its place.

Since the controller will transmit no more current than our solar panel, the solar cables we have will be perfect for transferring this current from controller to the battery. We secure the "plus" cable with a fuse holder (the same as in the case of the connection between the solar panel and the controller), and the minus is connected directly to the battery. Both cables end with ring connectors, which we're able to crimp perfectly thanks to a carefully made investment in a cable crimper.

Labeled wires are the enemy of any electric chaos.

Since the battery itself can draw a much greater current than the controller can provide, we must use a thicker wire (16 mm²) to ground it. The metal wall of the car is perfect for this task, in which, if necessary, we drill a hole in which we place the bolt on which we mount a ring connector with our grounding wire and screw the bolt preceded by a washer.

4. Fuse panel according to the technical specification, can accept a current of up to 100 or 150 amperes, so we need to use a wire that is as thick as the battery ground, i.e. with a cross-section of 16 mm². It can be very useful to separate the wire connecting it to the battery with a circuit breaker (interrupts current flow in case of overcurrent and is reusable unlike a fuse) – with a rated current about 25-30% higher than maximum current of all devices connected to the fuse panel). Finally the same effect can be obtained by disconnecting all the fuses plugged into the fuse panel itself.

Big fuse panel on the left and not so big ground bar on the right.

Its location should be considered together with the location of the negative bus bar for all our devices (if the fuse panel does not have one). Since we may end up with quite an amount of cables, it is worth providing them with the clearest and the shortest possible path.

Like the controller, the fuse box should be mounted in an easily accessible place.

5. Negative bus bar should also be mounted in an easily accessible place in case we want to add a new device to our system in the future. We connect the bar to the minus of our leisure battery with a thick grounding cable. Similarly to the controller and fuse box, it can be screwed to the vertical wall (e.g. inner side wall of the cabinet).

6. Devices (including a 12 V socket) are connected with the positive to the fuse panel and the negative to the ground bar. Of course, first, we deeply reflect upon appropriate arrangement of all the sockets and devices in the space of our mobile home. Thanks to the threaded 12 V socket, you can easily mount it in a car's wall panel by gently drilling a hole. If the socket is planned far from the fuse panel, it's most convenient to run the cable along the walls and the ceiling – behind the panels. For this reason it's a good idea to buy slightly thicker wires, since the highest temperatures will exist in the space between the panels and the car's walls.

Power plant in its full glory.

*Twelve-volt socket screwed to the wall panel
– painted in the same color as the wall,
it becomes almost invisible.*

*Twelve-volt socket screwed to the wall panel
– painted in the same color as the wall,
it becomes almost invisible.*

For the last time, we cross all possible fingers and close our circuit. Of course, starting from the end:

1. Make sure that the battery is grounded, and then press all the fuses in the fuse panel (and switch the circuit breaker, if installed).

2. Push the fuse between the battery and controller into the fuse holder. The controller should start working and await the advent of solar powers.

3. Push the fuse between the controller and the solar panel into the fuse holder.

This is how we become blissful observers of the beauty of nature, which makes us forget about electricity bills, burn notes with bank account numbers of energy suppliers, spontaneously call the whole family, hug your friends or your neighbor's cat, to express breathtaking admiration and satisfaction at this huge step towards... independence.

9. BED - CHEST

A BED ON WHICH YOU CAN EASILY SIT
AND UNDER WHICH YOU CAN HIDE
ALL YOUR STUFF

WHY: If we do not want to feel like a sardine in a can in our campervan, and we don't plan to transport a lot of equipment with us, a low profile bed will not only be enough to build a large luggage space under it, but above all it will give us something extremely important for a comfortable everyday life: s p a c e.

HOW IT WORKS: A full-size mattress will lay on a frame fitted with slats ("ribs"). In case of need, we'll be able to tilt this frame upwards so that a spacious cargo area will appear before our eyes – it will contain everything that we do not need on a daily basis, and which we have access to without getting out of the campervan.

WHAT WE NEED:
1. Mattress: 200 cm long, 90 cm wide and about 10 to 12 cm thick (minimum recommended thickness for a comfortable sleep).
2. Planks (preferably of the "tongue-and-groove" type) at least 12 mm thick and 12 cm wide – two for each side of the chest, so the total height will be about 24 cm. This dimension must be matched to the thick-

ness of the mattress so that the upper plank prevents it from sliding off the bed. The lengths given below must of course be slightly increased depending on the thickness of your planks:

• 2 side walls: 2 × 200 cm – 2 pieces (top and bottom)

   • 1 front wall: 2 × 90 cm – 2 pieces (top and bottom)

   • 1 rear wall: 2 × 90 cm - 2 pieces (top and bottom)

• reinforcement of the structure in the center of the chest: 2 × 90 cm – 2 pieces (at least 1 piece)

3. Wood blocks for legs: 4 × 4 × 18 cm – 6 pieces (they will protrude about 1.5 cm from the bottom to allow ventilation of the contents of the chest).

4. Long slats mounted on the inner perimeter of the chest – will rest on the legs of the chest. The frame of the bed will rest on these slats and provide support when tilting the frame. All slats are at least 1.2 cm thick and the same width as the legs of the chest (i.e. at least 4 cm). The lengths of these slats are just a bit smaller than the dimensions of the chest: 2 × 200 cm and 2 × 90 cm. When tilting the frame, the mattress will naturally fall over behind the bed. If such a scenario does not suit our expectations (e.g. it causes a collision with objects behind), it can be easily prevented by installing one wider slat. Then, when tilting the frame, you have to pull it slightly towards you. In this way, the mattress will fall on the wider slat and will wait there until we use the chest. The side slats and the central one running across the inner part of the chest will become rails for moving the bed frame. They'll also prevent the frame from falling inside the chest.

After tilting the frame with the mattress, pull it slightly towards you so that the mattress safely falls on the back "shelf" inside the chest.

5. Bed slats: 90 × 6 × 1.2 cm (14 pieces) – stiff version (elastic ones will start to creak after some time and weaken the structure) can be purchased in a hardware store + 2 slats for connecting the bed slats: 200 × 4 × 1.5 cm. This will create a bed frame that can be lifted.
6. Wood varnish.
7. Screws.
8. Felt for the legs of the chest.

TOOLS:
- woodworking jigsaw
- handheld saw/circular saw for wood (optional for your convenience)
- belt sander or orbital sander for wood

HOW TO DO IT: Finally, we measure the mattress and add at least 1 cm of extra length and width, so that the mattress falls easily after each use of the chest. It will also allow us to wrap the mattress with, for example, a blanket, the folded edges of which will fit under the mattress thanks to this additional space. Screw the walls of the chest to the legs, making sure that the legs protrude about 1.5 cm from the bottom. After all the walls with the legs are screwed together, we strengthen the structure in the center with additional planks that will divide our luggage compartment into two zones. If you plan to hide longer items, you can use only one instead of two boards dividing the chest in half. Then, along the inner perimeter of the chest, place the slats flat on the legs, on which the frame with bed slats will rest, and screw them on. Finally, we put two bed frame slats on them, to which we screw the bed slats. We use two long slats, so it will be a half frame, but after screwing the bed slats, the structure will be strong enough to create a solid frame for the mattress. An interesting circumstance appears here, as the spacing between the ribs allows you to look and even reach for smaller items from the chest without lifting the entire frame with the mattress (just slightly tilt a part of the mattress) – it's worth taking this into account and making one or two gaps between the bed slats large enough to pull out, for example, a typical-sized juice carton, or a small jar.

The whole structure is varnished twice to protect our work from moisture and other unwanted events for many years of happy sleep anywhere in the world.

Thanks to the ventilation from the bottom, we won't suffocate anyone or anything in the chest.

10. TOILET - TABLE - CAJÓN!

COMPOSTING TOILET WORTH A GRAND, AND AN EVERY DAY ELEGANT TABLE WITH ... A MUSIC FEATURE

WHY: Many van life enthusiasts instinctively reached for the vessel they had at hand when they found themselves in a sudden need. In addition, there's no more unpleasant sight than a traveler getting out of his fancy camper van to indulge in this lighter need in the nearby bushes. The accumulation of events of the latter type leads to a situation in which stopping even for a moment in the parking lot and opening the door takes away the whole enjoyment of such a lifestyle. Simply put, this stench is unbearable. After supplying my campervan with resources that fully meet these natural needs, I did not even once want to waste time looking for a suitable place, so if you feel similar, then I encourage you to solve both situations quite simply.

HOW IT WORKS: Some wise people wisely pointed out that by separating the effect of both "activities" into separate containers, we avoid the occurrence of a phenomenon that's not only environmentally unfriendly, but above all causes an unacceptable smell. Unfortunately, this someone wanted a thousand dollars for this solution. At that moment, a certain idea spoke to me: everything is an inspiration, a development or merely a modification of what has already been invented. Thus, as long as our creation is not a perfidious copy of what already exists, it has the right to its own, separate existence. Due to the small space, the most optimal solution turns out to be the purchase of an ultra-cheap toilet in the form of a container with a flap at the top with a toilet seat and placing an elegant wooden box on it, which not only creates a perfect camouflage, but also acts as a "ventilation chamber". In this way, the whole device is as small as possible, and after removing the covering, we have more space to sit comfortably in and do the thing. The interior of the toilet bin is equipped with a solid rubbish bag and poured in about five handfuls of crushed coconut fiber – a little known alternative to peat used in plant breeding. The coconut fiber is poured with 200-300 milliliters of water and thoroughly mixed – enough to stop it from dusting during mixing, and not too much, so that excessive moisture does not create an environment favorable to the development of undesirable natural creations (eg fungi). After each use, we cover the lid of the container with something leaving a slight opening. In this way, we ensure the air exchange inside, necessary for the removal of moisture, and above all the smell, which, even with each use, will resemble moist soil rather than the classic, unpleasant "smells". How will this air exchange happen? The casing that we slide over the toilet will have an opening sucking air inwards from the bottom. On the other hand, the drilled hole at the top of the rear wall of this housing will discharge the air with the help of a fan mounted in that hole. From the moment you use it for the first time, the fan will work tirelessly 24 hours a day, so it must be very quiet. Finally, the sucked air is discharged outside the car through a flexible ventilation hose (in my van, after removing the inner panel of the left wall, it turned out that there's a ventilation hole behind the wheel arch, through which the hose can be led outside). It's said that you have to wait up to a month for the composting process to start, and in practice we'll replace such a bag every 7–14 days by simply throwing it into a mixed waste container or burying its contents deep in the ground (if we are sure of the legality of such action in a given place). After each use of the toilet, it's worth shaking it a little to help the coconut fiber take action.

The above solution to need "number two" works great in case of both genders, but only when we have mastered the art of separating this need from a smaller, albeit equally important, "number one". If it's any consolation, this art must be mastered even by rock climbers, hanging several hundred meters above the ground, so as not to be cursed by the group of climbers beneath. I won't get into details, but you may find this anecdote encouraging each time to a successful completion of the task – human life may depend on it!

Need "number one" can be satisfied in case of men quite easily by using a large 5 or 8 liter water bottle, the purchase of which often becomes an indispensable part of campervan life. Of course, we dress the bottle in an elegant packaging, as it will become part of the interior design of our home on the wheels. Women can also take advantage of this option with a special funnel, although such a complicated procedure in such a small space may already require preliminary acrobatic skills. There are also unisex "funnels" with a permanent connection to the container, but these containers are quite small. The most convenient solution for women is to implement the design described here with a separator for the "first programme" built into the toilet, draining liquids into a separate container. This requires more work and space in the van, but the comfort of living will definitely be absolutely worth it.

Anyway, the elegantly enclosed toilet is invisible on a daily basis, and even serves as a small table. However, if we use slightly thicker wood to build it, we can transform our work into a percussion instrument known from the flamenco world of music, called *cajón* – a wooden box with a sound hole. For the full potential of such an instrument, it remains only to mount the strings stretched against the wall opposite to the one with the hole and gracefully shout: *eeessooo!*

WHAT WE NEED:

1. A bucket-toilet, i.e. a container with a flap at the top and a toilet seat (at least 20 liters). Dimensions: length and height 37 cm, width 34 cm.

2. Plywood (preferably already waterproof): minimum thickness 4 mm – to cover the toilet on all sides except the bottom. We adjust the dimensions adequately to the toilet purchased.

3. Slats that will be used as the frame of the structure – at least 1.5 cm thick. Dimensions adequate to the dimensions of the cut plywood + 1 cm more for the legs (ventilation from the bottom).

4. Wooden blocks: 7 × 7 × 2 cm (2 pieces) – we'll make holes in them for placing the fan and the venti-

lation hose. They will serve as fasteners for these elements.

5. Nails – for an elegant connection of slats with plywood.

6. Wood glue – for sealing the whole structure.

7. Screws – for mounting the fan and the ventilation hose (8 pieces).

8. Wood varnish.

9. Very quiet computer fan (it's good to take 1 spare), dimensions: 4 × 4 × 1 cm, noise level: 15-18 dB, maximum speed: 4000 rpm (speed regulation feature recommended).

10. EPDM rubber: 3 mm thick – it can be the same that we used for the solar panel mounting brackets, although you can look for something softer for even better tightness and reduction of possible vibrations caused by the fan.

11. Polyester felt or a piece of soft material with dimensions: 20 × 1 × 0.2 cm (2 pieces) – for tight fitting of the fan and the ventilation hose in the holes in the wooden blocks.

12. Ventilation hose (e.g. polyurethane): flexible, microbe resistant, reinforced with metal spiral. Dimensions: 4 cm diameter and 1 meter long.

TOOLS:
- woodworking jigsaw
- handheld saw/circular saw for wood (optional for your convenience)
- belt sander or orbital sander for wood
- drill and a hole saw/hole cutter (4-5 cm diameter).
- cross screwdriver

HOW TO DO IT: We put pieces of plywood on the bucket-toilet and measure the final dimensions of the side walls of the box. In order to easily take the box on and off during everyday use, I recommend adding a few millimeters of space on each side – struggling with a wooden box during "an emergency" is not exactly as fun as it may seem now. We measure the height of the walls taking into account not only 1-1.5 cm of clearance from the bottom, but definitely more at the top for the slats that form the frame of the entire wooden structure. The extra space at the top will also be needed to leave the toilet flap slightly open for constant air exchange. After cutting 4 side and 1 upper wall, we cut 4 longer slats for the legs and 4 shorter ones to connect them at the top. Next we make sure that everything fits, because in a moment there will be no turning back. We cover the contact surfaces with wood glue and nail everything together. First, you can hammer the nails halfway, brush the surfaces with glue and then finish the nails. This way the elements won't slip during the precise nailing process. It is best to start with the side walls, to finally glue and nail the more or less perfectly fitting upper part, and sand any imperfections later with the already dried wood glue, which likes to expand on all sides, perfectly filling any gaps in the structure.

A hole for the ventilation hose is drilled at the top edge of one of the walls (for the best possible ventilation) – as high as possible, i.e. right under the upper, horizontal slat. The diameter of the hole should be adjusted to the diameter of the fan that we decided to buy.

In wooden block number 1, we cut a square hole the size of our fan, adding 1-2 millimeters more on each side for the felt. Thanks to this, the fan can be replaced at any

The toilet's ventilation system is so perfect that we can eat right off it. On the counter, that is, to be exact.

time by pushing the old one out with a finger and inserting a new one with a slight resistance. In addition, we cut a small groove from the inside to the outside of the block, which will be used to lead the fan cable out. Then, from thick rubber or other foam, we cut two gaskets the size of our wooden tiles. Said cable groove can therefore alternatively be made by cutting one of the gaskets.

In the 2nd wooden block, we cut a round hole matching the diameter of our ventilation hose plus 1-2 millimeters more for felt – thanks to it, it'll be easy to install the hose and, if necessary, remove it.

The assembly process is identical to the procedure for a possible replacement of the fan: we put the gasket and the plate no.1 to the opening in the box and screw everything to the box with four screws. Then we insert the fan, lead out the cable (with a groove or notch in the seal).

Wooden blocks connect the fan and the ventilation hose
to each other. A computer fan has probably
a hundred more hidden uses.

On top of this we put the second gasket and the 2nd wooden block, which we screw to block number one with four screws, but in a slightly different place, so that they don't meet the screws of the block number one. With a rotating movement, we insert the ventilation hose into the hole in plate number two – here we have to be careful not to insert it too far, which will result in a loud grinding of the fan propeller blades. The other end of the hose is squeezed through the hole that we drill in the wall panel – exactly in front of the vent in the car body. The end of the hose is led out as far as possible and secured against any visits of rodents (e.g. with an aluminum/plastic grille) and even insects (e.g. with an additional piece of mosquito net).

For convenience, the fan cable can be connected to the cable from the fuse box using the simplest switch that can be mounted (e.g. with double-sided tape or Velcro tape) to the wall of the toilet box – right next to plate number one. The cable going further can be wrapped around the hose and fastened every several centimeters with a cable tie. Theoretically, the hose will be hidden behind the box all the time, so this solution should not hurt the eyes of even the most sensitive aesthetes. However, the sound of even such a quiet fan can disturb the blissful quiet at night in beautiful natural circumstances, so you can consider mounting the fan in the wall.

While driving, the toilet itself can go on its journey on the floor of our camper van (not to mention the possible flight of the toilet with all its contents during the unfortunate rolling down the slope of the road). Therefore, it's worth preventing any movement of the toilet at all.

Every day a table with a tied leg, so that it doesn't run away too far while driving.

A simple and effective solution is tying a piece of elastic rope to the car body (in mine there was just a hole next to it), and on the other hand tying the loop and putting it on the leg of the box. Not that I didn't warn you: this solution protects against traveling on the floor, but does not protect against a possible flight through the living space of our house on wheels.

Toilet "ready to rock".

II. HEATING AND COOLING

STRIKINGLY SIMPLE SOLUTIONS WITH STRIKINGLY GOOD RESULTS

WHY: Sometimes one unpleasant element can spoil a whole, altogether very positive experience, and even discourage us from continuing our journey. For example, it could be a few days that are too cold or too hot on a highly planned, very long trip. It's worth preparing for such circumstances and thus ensuring not only physical but also mental comfort of the entire undertaking.

HOW IT WORKS: In addition to a good sleeping bag, an electric blanket turns out to be a great solution for warming the body. Simply put it's an ordinary blanket with a piece of heated wire inside and although it warms up quite slowly, I can assure you that after a few hours it may turn out to be too hot for us.

For cooling, on the other hand, a properly placed and aimed small fan turns out to work quite well. When placed in front of slightly open doors, it will blow cooler air from the outside (and the air outside will always be cooler on hot days). While the noise it makes may irritate us a bit over time, we'll certainly appreciate this "noise of coolness" during any heatwave.

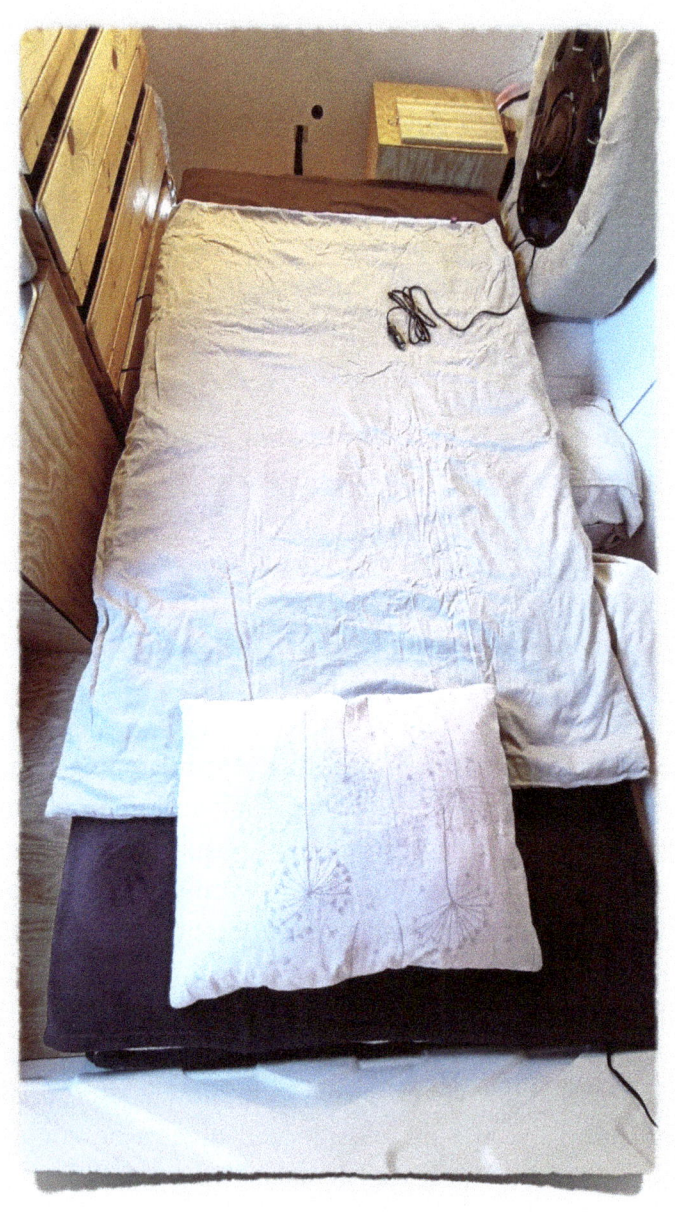

A blanket dressed in a duvet cover - ready for electrifying bed actions.

WHAT WE NEED:

1. Electric blanket: 12 V, at least 40 W (3-4 A) for one person – size at your discretion (minimum 100 × 140 cm) + mummy sleeping bag (preferably flexible, i.e. adjusting to the body position).

2. Fan with a rotor diameter of at least 12 cm, 5 V power supply (with USB plug) or 12 V power supply (with plug for car socket): quiet (!), with a handle for easy mounting, preferably with a built-in battery (it's easier to mount it the proper place, without dragging the cable).

HOW TO DO IT: Without going into the laws of physics, the fact is that heat escapes upwards. Therefore, it's better to put an electric blanket on the bed than cover yourself with it. Next we slide into a mummy-shaped sleeping bag, which allows the body to be completely "submerged". Thanks to this, in the most extreme situations, the only unheated element of our body will be the nose, which by the way has a pretty good heating system for the inhaled air. Additionally, you can cover yourself with a blanket from above, which will prevent heat from escaping – the heat which we also emit as a side effect of supporting life functions.

The only downside to this solution is that the living space is not heated, which would require a lot more energy and noise. If you want to comfortably spend time in a motor-home during cold days, you need to think about a fuel-powered heater (with a good silencer).

Cooling, on the other hand, will consist in replacing all the air inside. in a position that offers the least resistance to the air flowing into the van. If our location is not conducive to the full opening of all doors, a wedge from the sink cabinet will be useful here, thanks to which you can leave the rear door hatch slightly open (of course, if your car has a hatch that opens upwards). The most important thing in hot weather is to have the car ajar at both ends to give a chance to create a through draft.

The fan only blows reasonably when it's placed in a reasonable place – that probably sounds reasonable.

12. LIGHTING AND DIMMING

THE MIRACLE OF TECHNOLOGY:
LED (LIGHT EMITTING DIODE)

WHY: Living in a motorhome is a great opportunity to live according to the natural cycle of the day – we go to bed at sunset and get up at sunrise. For those who prefer to stay awake more than sleep, LEDs will be of help. Dozens or even hundreds of LEDs. They consume so little electricity that you don't really need to limit yourself on this one. And if we like to sleep longer, or simply want some privacy in the middle of the day, then perfectly matched curtains in the windows will protect us from glaring rays of the sun or curious eyes.

HOW IT WORKS: A cable with lots of LEDs located around the living space will effectively illuminate the whole area, although for a greater effect and atmosphere, you can think of additional spotlights (single, stronger LED).

Effective dimming, on the other hand, will be ensured by pieces of material well suited to the shape of each window, in which the edges will be sewn with magnets. This will allow us not only to put them on or take them off very easily, but it will also provide many options for partially covering the window. In addition, several magnets sewn along the top or bottom edge will allow us to roll the curtain when not in use.

WHAT WE NEED:

1. LED decorative lights on a wire (tape versions will leave an ugly trail on the ceiling): about 80-100 LEDs, powered with current of 5 V (via USB charger) or 12 V (directly from leisure battery), preferably with a remote control (if not available, we buy the most ordinary switch that we'll mount on the wire).

2. Fabric (e.g. velor upholstery, weight 300 g/m²) or foam (e.g. sleeping mat) if we need thermal insulation (then a large storage space will be needed when not in use). Dimensions in accordance with the needs of our windows. Best color will be the one that corresponds to the colors of our living space, which may not, of course, be the same as the car's external color – this in effect works against the camouflage of our camper van. A compromise can be achieved by sewing together two pieces of cloth with a lower fabric weight – the double fabric gets really heavy and harder to hold with magnets.

3. Magnets: 10 x 15 x 0.1 mm (although the 0.2 mm thick ones are much stronger) – with the above-mentioned fabric weight, you need to count the magnet every 10-15 cm around the perimeter of the window. Remember that when the curtain is open it's only held by a few magnets, so there must be enough of them to support the weight of the curtain.

4. Double-sided adhesive acrylic tape: length corresponding to the sum of the circumferences of all curtains.

5. Thread in the color of the fabric.

Uniform illumination with several dozen LEDs
– now we're always prepared for Christmas.

Additional atmospheric illumination of... a water tank
– with one but more powerful light emitting diode.

HOW TO DO IT: We start the installation of lighting by determining the path of the wire with LEDs, starting from the 12 V socket. Then we determine the location of a possible switch, if we have a LED version without a remote control. If so, cut the cable in the place where we plan to attach the switch to the wall, i.e. where it's most convenient for us to reach for it every day. According to the principle of "plus to plus, minus to minus", we screw the switch to the cable and attach it to the wall, eg with double-sided adhesive tape. We scrupulously shape the wire with LEDs into arched shapes and push it into the gaps behind the panels covering the walls and the ceiling.

It is best to start making curtains by temporarily attaching the fabric to the window with magnets and tracing the desired shape, and even marking the places where the magnets will be attached to the curtain. When cutting, remember to add at least 2 cm for the overlap, behind which the magnets will hide. To make the edges of the curtains slightly stiff, you can stick a double-sided adhesive tape around the curtain's perimeter, which you can also use to stick the magnets in the desired place. Thanks to these tapes, the curtain will stick better to the window, which will prevent possible light streams from entering at night, and will not reveal our presence inside (if we use a sufficiently thick fabric).

If we don't aspire to the main prize in the local seam-stresses competition, the hand-drawn, so-called straight stitch will do its job and absolutely not embarrass us, if we only plan to direct the overlap to the outside of the car window. Our tailoring imperfections will be covered from the outside by black window frames (the exception is the situation where our car window does not have such a frame). In addition, the needle can be threaded through the fabric even every 2 cm, which will allow for possible later verification of the number and location of the magnets.

It is very useful to sew in a few additional magnets along a line distant from the upper edge of the window by about 10 cm. Thanks to that, the curtain can be rolled up and "magnetized" to the upper frame of the window. The mentioned distance is best assessed by yourself after several attempts to roll the curtain as tight as possible.

If the metal structure of our motorhome is covered from the inside with all kinds of finishing elements, then we'll have to mount additional magnets to these elements. The presence of magnets in these places can be quite elegantly camouflaged, e.g. with a matt self-adhesive foil.

Curtain in "covering mode".

Slightly open in the corner.

Half open.

Rolled up.

THE END
IS
THE BEGINNING

Every end is a beginning of something new. So it's time to hit the road. No matter where. What matters is that it's the road ahead. Enjoy the true freedom of being closer to the world, living where even the most expensive hotel cannot stand. Stop living in a world within concrete walls and start being a part of it. Start a life more aware of how little we need to meet all the needs of our everyday life. Meet people with whom we can feel the connection with just one glance. People who will inspire us to continue our journey or those whom we ourselves will inspire.

Let's go!

Milton Keynes UK
Ingram Content Group UK Ltd.
UKHW021324280524
443385UK00044B/982